Virgo, the Wordmaker

E.V.E's Heartbreak

Also by Alphonso Taylor

Sexual Freedom: Urban Erotic Poetry
Bible of an Alligator: A Collection of Poems
Bible of an Owl: A Collection of Poems

Virgo, the Wordmaker

E.V.E's Heartbreak

By:

Alphonso Taylor

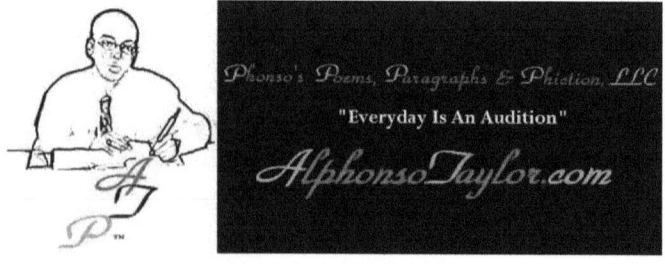

Copyright © 2009 by Alphonso Taylor

All rights reserved. No part of this publication may be reproduced, stored in a retrieval system or transmitted in any form or by any means, electronic, mechanical, photocopying, recording, scanning, or otherwise, without the written permission of the author.

Artwork & Cover Design By: Alphonso Taylor

Model On Cover: Tiffany 'Parris Jewel' Parker

Photo By: Donato Sebastian

Art Advisor & Back Cover Photo By: Shelton D. Taylor
Text & Composition: Assuanta Howard

ISBN13: 978-0-615-31187-6

Printed in the United States of America

This book is dedicated to my parents

Alphonso 'Al' Pierce, Jr. and

Cheryl R. Taylor

You are the great, unusual god and goddess who raised a king to the best of his ability.

Your courage will always live in me as I love both of you to death!

Acknowledgements

First and foremost, I will like to thank God Almighty for blessing me with the gift of writing on a distinct, versatile level. Through the grace, I see an entire vision in the business of self-publishing. I'm grateful to perform and sell my art to different cultures and age groups of people. I might just be better off as an author, than actor. To my wonderful parents, Cheryl R. Taylor and Alphonso 'Al' Pierce, Jr. Mom, you know I'll always love you dearly despite our problems. I did what a son was suppose to do and protected you. I never wanted to disrespect you as we've been to hell and back. I'm so delighted to see you happy now. **FUCK THE PAST AND NEVER AGAIN!** Dad, I don't know what made you take me as your own from when I was a tot to a man and I'm glad you did. I'm proud to be an Alphonso for life. I just want to be as brave and powerful as you with skilled hands and trade, passing our name to one of my own. I just don't know when I'll grant you with that wish… Definitely, I want to receive it one day and I'm gracious to produce and reproduce. To my distant sister, Shanté M. Taylor. I trained you to be tough and I see you've shown it thoroughly. I just want to reunite our bond to how it used to be. Love you! Until then, I'm the happiest uncle of your daughter, my niece, Sikia N. Taylor. She's such an angelic princess. I'm glowing to see her walk, talk and laugh. To my uncle, Shelton D. Taylor. I'm honored to see we had both gotten out. Although we might go our separate ways, you still work for me, **BITCH!** LOL! All contracts are on and can get cancelled, if not valued … You're right, man. It's like we can't fully escape all the bullshit because we don't look like a lot of these mutherfuckas out here. I know we have each other's back. To my favorite, little cousin, Shelton J. Taylor. I want to see him grow up to be an artist or anything he puts his mind to. To uncle, David L. Taylor for all your former and future support. Thank you so much for promoting your nephew. I owe you from the third book. You're pretty much one of my inspirations of how a man shall carry himself in this crazy and stereotypical world. To the whole Taylor family despite hardships. **THE TAYLORS ARE NOT FAILURES!** A big shout-out goes to Mike Davis.

Before I can thank anyone else, I must highly thank my friend and home girl, Tiffany 'Parris Jewel' Parker for making this possible. Sweetie, I can just remember us sitting in class at junior high school in our uniforms and glasses, being nerds. LMAO! Well, I'm not afraid to admit that I'm still one in the coolest way ever. I always knew you are beautiful and it still shows 12 years later. You're definitely modeling material and I love your SEXY ASS! Muah! I can't believe you blessed me with a cover and soon, a story... Incredible! To my best friend, Michael 'Mike' Dorsey. Man, what can I say? You're my brother I've never had for almost two decades, since elementary to the turn of century and a lot of history. There were times I looked up to you and you're the youngest. You're my homie forever. CONGRATS, on becoming a father with your wife, my sister-n-law, Cierra Kindred or shall I say Mrs. Dorsey? I'm so proud of y'all. Looks like I'll have another niece or my new, first nephew to spoil. To the rest of the M.A.S.T Villains and S.E.C. Records for continuing to do y'all thing. Maybe one day, we can all get back in the studio and take over Southeast for real, musically. To my homie, Jamar Biscoe. You're pretty much one of the few friends I made in college and I'm cool we're still tight up to this day. Man, when you're really ready to do these projects, don't hesitate to holler at me. Meanwhile, I have to do me. I appreciate all the times we did our thing on the DC club scene. To everybody from the Anacostia neighborhood who was always cool with me. It's pretty much one of the best neighborhoods I lived in. At last but never least, to my Wagfest family for tremendous support. It all starts with Shani Greene Dowdell for having me on your Blogtalk radio show, *Erotica Gone Wild*. Later, it became a great invitation to meeting Kerry E. Wagner, the founder. Felecia Trotter, Nola Love, Bonnie Calloway, April Howenstein, Ivanna Howles, Naiomi Pitre, Tra Verdejo, Gregory 'Black Tiger' Sargent, Sapphire, and many more. Assuanta Collins, I have to thank you for opening my eyes to better publishing directions and for making Asta Publications my new home. I appreciate you on a professional, networking, and social status. To everyone who always had believed in and always will believe in me, from the womb to the tomb. Family is valuable! Hell yeah!

Introducing E.V.E.

Well, here we are again. This time, I'm somewhat happy with a new breed of emotions. It's been quite, successful phases from good, evil to sexual. Still, I never thought in a million years, I could experience at this moment of my life, my first heartbreak. The feeling is genuine, giving the side of me too emotional...

I remember during my senior year of college, I was taking Literary and Advanced Writing II. We just got finished reading short plays and were starting Poetry. One night in class, a classmate asked my favorite English teacher, Dr. Williams of her definition of a poet. Actually, I was defining myself like when a superhero first receives powers from the beginning of a dramatic event. Dr. Williams said a poet comes across as a rhyme genius, an extraordinary writer or wordmaker. A wordmaker?

Since then, the name stood with me. I just needed to link it with something, so it could have its unique sound. I already knew it was going to be for an upcoming book. I was always interested in astrology and how it relates to my existence. Soon, I would become so fascinated with my magnificent zodiac sign, the Virgo.

Virgo the virgin, an earth and feminine sign, is the sixth sign of the tropical constellation. The sun shines in Virgo between Aug. 23 and Sept. 22, though it can change depending on year. The Virgo appears to be a delicate girl or older female holding sheaves of wheat, which symbolizes wisdom garnered in the fields of experience. As the true virgin, most Virgos are shy and perfectionists like a virgin waiting to give herself to the pure lover. Also, Virgos are idealistic and ruled by planet, Mercury.

Failure can harden me into a cynic. I'm my own worst critic on the effect of discriminating nature. I have a tendency to present cleanliness, hygiene and great order. Sometimes, I feel shielded towards friendships and relationships because I'm not that trustworthy of others. I can lack in some things and make up for them in other alternatives. It takes a lot to make me upset and when I am, I can have a sharp tongue.

The most known characteristics of Virgos; we're freaks in bed, like to be dominant, unforgettable, always want the last word, make good partners and parents, have a strong eye for information, worrisome, intellectual, and affectionate. Somebody loves a Virgo right now. Also, Virgos make good fashion designers, editors, writers and more. We're more compatible with Pisces, Taurus, and Capricorns. We're less compatible with Aries, Libras, and Aquarius and in my case, Sagittarius.

I was born September 13, 1983 in Southeast, Washington DC, also known as capital city. Although I get fed up of the quarrel that goes on in my hometown, I'll always love DC. Because I have worked hard to strengthen my art, I can now say I'm an incredible and professional wordmaker. Before I started penning books, I used to try and be a rapper having freestyle sessions, which are called ciphers. I'm not really a people's person, so I believe I stand out amongst others because I'm different in my own unique style. Having a percent of arrogance is my motivation against negativity fallen at me.

I don't have to prove myself to no one. Competing with or hating another human being has never been my strategy as it's a dumb, rat race. I'm sick of the job hunting and working for folks to be stable. Soon, I'm giving myself before or at the age of 30 to finally get stuff on the right track to go in business for myself and work for me. You need a job? If it's a miracle, I will like to share my success with the woman of my dreams for the rest of my life. Just settle down, raise and have a clan. Most women, I wanted to get serious with or we were like that, wasn't on the same page. It goes for some of the ones I just meet too. I'm always put on some waitlist until a breakup. That explains why my chest hurts, feeling like an icebox. I'm chilly! I'm a Virgo who once thought I found the perfect woman for me, but was mistaken. A lot of men are not into thick, voluptuous ladies, but I'm attracted to and am crazy about phat women.

When I get my erotic drive back in full boost, I want to ignite that seductive temperature between me and a sexy, sophisticated woman. Then, we make love over and over again in the afterglow. I enjoy food so much like I do women and sex. I had to write about what makes me hungry. LOL! I'm only 25 and sometimes I feel like I should be 50. Since I was a kid, I have had the genre of an old man. I'm the oldest and first born with a sibling who has the same month and day of my birthday, five years apart. When I rest from a day of progress, I sometimes have spirits in my sleep because I'm clouded with ideas ahead. Every now and then, I have to redeem myself to see where I've been, where I'm at now, and where I'm going. Overcoming so many obstacles in my path and I'm still vigorous, I'll always have tears of triumph at a given notice.

E.V.E. is the virgin, female representation of the author of this book. Because Alphonso has a sudden heartbreak, *she* shares his same sympathy. She can't take it anymore and wants to voice her truth of what makes her tick. E.V.E., *her* name is three, absolute characteristics of him as a Virgo. Get ready to meet E.V.E. Please, enjoy!

A Virgo Rhyme

But modest Virgo's rays give polished parts,
And fill men's breasts with honesty and arts;
No tricks for gain, nor love of wealth dispense,
But piercing thoughts and winning eloquence.

— **Manilius**

Virgo, the Wordmaker

♍

Capital City (I Love DC)	1
The Wordmaker	4
Cipher	5
I Stand Out	6
Percent of Arrogance	7
Rat Race	8
The Wheat: Talk to Myself	9
Virgin (Alphonso, the Virgo)	12
E.V. E'S Heartbreak	15
Job Hunt	19
Work For Me	21
Waitlist	25
Tug of Women: Younger -Alphonso - Older	27
Virgo and a Woman	39
Leave My Beauty Alone	40
Phat Women	42

Seductive Temperature	47
Afterglow	49
Food Poem	52
Old Man Genre	54
Born First	55
Spirits in My Sleep	56
Redemption	57
Tears of Triumph	58

Effeminate

Alphonso Taylor

Capital City (I Love DC)

♏

I'm that MC
  from DC
I hustle my words in poetry

That MC
  from DC
I hustle my words in poetry

That MC
From DC
I hustle my words in poetry
Hustle my words in poetry
Hustle my words in poetry

SOUTHEAST, NORTHEAST, NORTHWEST, SOUTHWEST…DC is the best, BEST

SOUTHEAST, NORTHEAST, NORTHWEST, SOUTHWEST…DC is the best, BEST

SOUTHEAST, NORTHEAST, NORTHWEST, SOUTHWEST…DC is the best, BEST

DC is the best, BEST
ALWAYS be the best, YES

Virgo, the Wordmaker

I'm from that Capital City
The honest hustle, grind and gritty
Where anyone can get popped swiftly
Sometimes known as the Chocolate
The bullshit and Congress
We got all type of residents
The White House, crib of the president
FINALLY, I'm glad to have in my hometown, a BLACK PRESIDENT
All of DC including Southeast ain't that bad
Numerous HIV stats
Drugs and high crime rates
As the cops roll down the avenues
Through some hoods of ash
We have the greatest hoes, dope fiends and winos
They seem weird, but they keep the ghetto live though
The town of R&B and Go-Go, the sound of Chuck Brown
Designed by George Washington and Charles P. L'Enfant
Along with Benjamin Banneker and Andrew Ellicott
The graffiti on jacked up Metro trains, bus stations, and stops
Okay public schools
Most of our stores and carry-outs owned by Asians
Home of the Redskins and Wizards
Gallery Place-Chinatown, get your grub and movie on
The party spots are Adam's Morgan and Georgetown
All up in the happy hour
We have the best girls; just go around UDC and Howard
The homecomings are never jive
Jeannie Jones KYS, PGC 95
The birthday bash at the Verizon Center
WHUR, the hottest shows and concerts at Constitution Hall
Take a walk downtown on the Mall
Historic for the Monument, Supreme Court and museums
Memorials, parades, and summer jams
This is the city of dreams
Where he gave his famous speech, Dr. Martin Luther King
On the wharf, it's the Spirit of Washington
Even though we're not a state
We look out for terrorism and hate
Our men and women are always being stereotyped
General Hospital
Lockdown of its jail system

Alphonso Taylor

Can we get a decent mayor and council member
After a while, this city, a lot of people want to leave
I may wanna leave too
 Its closer to VA and MD
There is no other place I really rather be
I'll always love DC

Virgo, the Wordmaker

The Wordmaker

♍

The wordmaker
An instigator
for my freedom of speech to fight
to stay original, right
A voice in public speaking
Spoken word
Cheap verse of the Absurd
Can I buy a vowel
A moving dictionary
remixing adjectives and nouns
Got Milk as in fake compounds
Antonyms, synonyms, homonyms
Don't drink it with acronyms
Literate and hooked on Phonics
Can't preach Ebonics
How can I be the topic
and I never been sentenced
I'ma run-on, Essay
You need to check your spelling and thesis
I'm not in clichés
He say, she say
My common language is Inglé
I'ma Mister, tongue twister, listener
Metaphor, simile
It sounds like hyper bowl, Hyperbole
To my words just listen
Find me as a definition
never ending a poem with a preposition
Perhaps…

Alphonso Taylor

Cipher

♍

It's the cipher
This is where the writer
Don't answer to the piper
I can't be nervous
Ready to serve these clowns with a purpose
The circle gets quiet waiting for me to spit
Rock the mic and scene to rip
Some fans say I look like NaS
Like in Belly, I was getting it on with T-Boz
Made you look
Still, I'm overlooked
As I got my opponents hooked
Hyping the crowd
The way Eminem did in 8 Mile
It's a free world
Me against the world, boys and girls
A stand up man
Playing the victory is my band
After the sessions, I get mad play from groupies
The fellas upset, please don't shank or shoot me
I'm not a poet shopping for a demo
Inquiring minds ask you
Have any labels yet snatched you
I look them in the face and say I don't battle
I just don't really freestyle...

Virgo, the Wordmaker

I Stand Out

♍

A short dude
with a cool attitude
Hated by many, loved by few
I stand out

Slightly above average
Gifted and talented
Never too easily challenged
I stand out

Don't always get respect to credit I deserve
Sometimes get on people's nerves
keeping my balls and my word
I stand out

Had to cut loose some friends
A lot of cliques, I never fit in
They back stab me over trend
I stand out

Struggling, but not broke
Usually seen as a ghost
Stay to myself the most
I stand out

Pay the price for being such a nice guy
To do the right thing, I try
I do so much just to get by
I stand alone

Alphonso Taylor

Percent of Arrogance

♍

Badmouthing me
is cursing yourself
Stealing from me
is putting your life in debt
What's the text
Who's the best
As y'all bow to my shoestrings
All this hate got me seeing things
I'm already a celebrity
In my presence, it's always jealousy
I have the cold shoulder with dust
Fuck a popularity contest
I know my jock is big with so much clout
I don't need your weak paparazzi
Folks whom wishy-washy
I've done got a little cocky
Only God can stop me
I breeze on by with perseverance
Record this percent of arrogance
To embarrass me, you have no real surveillance
Spreading rumors, y'all got a lot of nerve
Stick a condom in your ear and fuck what you heard
WHEW, I'ma calm down and return to my normal self
I've finally liberated my mind

Virgo, the Wordmaker

Rat Race

♍

On your march, get set, GO
I want out
It has no face
Tired of the cat- and-mouse chase
Where's the rat in this race
I don't have to play catch up
To me, there's really no match up
With anyone, I'm in no competition
I always begin from the finish line
Working my way back to the start
Maybe, I'ma steady pacer
A machine of stride racer
Constantly, tiptoeing on eggshells
Jogging to stay on track
Running errands around it
to please everyone, but myself
A gold medal I suppose
The restricted Olympics
Let me pull to the side and catch my breath
Can't adjust to people's expected speed of me
I'm dashing through the meters
Who's getting me to the yards
What is wanted from me
No one really cares
I move like the tortoise versus the hare
Going up a questionable stair
to one day inhale the heavenly air

Alphonso Taylor

The Wheat: Talk to Myself

♍

Everyday, I'm learning to be the author of my own horoscopes. I kind of have a kinetic power to predict things and I'm not really psychic or astrological. It's this particular horoscope; I have come across a few times, which seems to only be talking to me. I can't fully remember what it says and on that note, I must have written my first horoscope. It goes like this, *"I always provide the shoulder for those to lean on, but where my helping hand is when I need it."* This pretty much describes my somewhat, anti-social being.

I find a lot of people come to me because they say, I'm easy to get along with and it's true to some extent, depending on the individuals. They run things by me, they feel cannot be shared with no one else because certain folks give a crazy impression. I'm looked at as cool of course, and very friendly. So, sometimes I have to be a sponge and absorb minerals of problems and frustrations thrown at me. I'm all eyes and ears serving as a counselor or philosopher to a good listener.

Before I'm anything in life, I'm always a realist first. I bring realism and logic in almost all situations. I can empathize with many peers and elders, garnered through the wheat of my life experiences. I try to offer words of encouragement, although I'm not the greatest in advice. I just look forward for my information to be in good use.

As I'm spreading love, I have to deal with my own troubles. Apparently, I talk to myself for some type of guidance. It seems, when I go to the same people who needed me, they're nowhere to be found. Just about everybody gets upset, huffing and puffing, if it's me to receive favors. Filled

Virgo, the Wordmaker

with lies of why they can't have my back. But, they continue to have the audacity of wanting me to be generous for free, based on the kindness of my heart. Forget that!

I guess it gets lonely because I'm tired of getting the short end of the stick. I go out of my way to actually rescue lives and feed hungry mouths, just so they can be against me to harm me? My charisma may be honest and welcoming, but don't EVER underestimate it. I'm further from feebleness. Now, I'm capable of growing thicker skin.

I'm still searching my identity for other usual features besides my baby face and small stature, which these goons think I'm a regular target of manipulation. Always feeling as if, they can take whatever from me and get away. Soon as I reveal the anguish bottled inside, then I'm the bad guy and you don't like me anymore, which I don't give a flying fuck. ***STAY GONE!*** You thought my nerdy exhibit is some walkover. You don't know I have the smarts from schools to the streets with a smidgen amount of hood credibility. I don't have to claim thug or gangster. I'm a soldier for the survival of the fittest. Every time I step out my house, its warfare in any form.

GODDAMNIT! *No*, I don't always have spare change, a dollar or change for dollar bills to cents. *No*, I don't know the directions to every place. *No*, you can't borrow my cellphone. *No*, I can't stop in my tracks to tell you what time it is. *No*, I can't watch this and that for you all the time because I have to attend to my belongings. I won't demonstrate every technique.

Can I get a break? Sometimes to be a Sumerian is pointless. I have to keep bonds superficial. Everything and everybody drops in and out of my circle. I don't know what's going to last anymore. An old instructor of mine told me that everything is bullshit and I thought I was the only one who felt that. To me, it's right. **EVERYTHING IS BULLSHIT.**

Alphonso Taylor

    There are only a handful of folks I can run to, so I can vent. I try my best not to relent. The profit of an outsider can be a blessing and disguise. I'm extra careful of what I say and do. It's like your statements and actions can get twisted and used as a setup to bring you down. Random scenarios are created out of my power. It's not in my genes to be about hurting anybody, but I'm not gonna let anybody hurt me.

    The older I get, there are so many reasons everybody wants to whack you. I used to believe them all. Somebody's got to be false. Corners and outlets are covered on my behalf as much as possible. It seems, I'm not greatly considered, until I'm completely or almost out of the picture. I'm done with breaking myself down to rest cases. No more guilt trips on me. Frequently, I have this reoccurring plan in my head and it doesn't sound like a bad idea to go M.I.A …

Virgo, the Wordmaker

Virgin (Alphonso, the Virgo)

♍

No one knows that female inside with me
Protecting my soul of bad pride with me
Against everything that wanna collide with me

Alphonso
the Virgo
The virgin must fight for a yes or no

Hard for me to open, cuz my fate has been broken
If I offer you my charm, appreciate the token
Stubbornness can take over and I'll be soft spoken

I hold on real tight to my integrity
In search for the life of longevity
Some circumstances lose my temper to virginity

Alphonso
the Virgo
The virgin must fight for a yes or no

It doesn't matter, what's my origin
I'm only human, got a sweet tooth for sin
When chaos gonna cease, so I can win

My brain runs hours per mile
From foes, I keep a low profile
NOT GOING NOWHERE, I'm here for awhile

So, me alive is how you have to bury
A man with a whole lot of joy and fury
Go thru great shit on Earth, but I'm ruled by Mercury

Alphonso the Virgo
The virgin must fight for a yes or no

E.V.E and Phonso, are they the same person

E.V.E and Phonso, are they the same Virgo

E.V.E and Phonso, are they the same virgin

Never forget me, cherish my fame
How I am the truth, far from lame
Tell me something new, everything sounds the same

I'm put on the edge
My strength is full fledge
To stay on top, I pray and I pledge

Don't be in a hurry of me to be critical
You become wishful, wish you didn't say ignoral
 Most of y'all are fake, very artificial

Until whenever, I'll be that buzzing mosquito
Making those big moves, incognito
The leader doing it his way like, Carlito

Alphonso the Virgo
The virgin must fight for a yes or no

Hey yo,
she goes by E.V.E
Effeminate, Virginal, Emotional
If you ain't rolling with her, SO!

ALPHONSO, THE VIRGO

Alphonso Taylor

E.V.E's Heartbreak

♍

My parents asked, when I'll give them grandkids
Some women, I had put in those bids
With the embryos, don't know what fault I did

All I have is my cousin and niece
Try to be to them a role model piece
Personal life, who'll keep me warm as a fleece

She gave me an 'E' because I'm sensitive as her

Got so many ladies that owe me sex
But, my last performances in sheets has been complex
Have I really loss my fuse and where do I start next

Once felt I was rewarded true love
It flew away from its nest like a dove
Now, I only rely on the ones from above

She gave me a 'V' believing I'm still young and fresh with a whole lot to give

Oh, it happens, again and again
Oh, it happens, again and again
Blow in the air, gone with the wind
Blown in the air, gone with the wind

Virgo, the Wordmaker

I saw a couple in the park locking hands
I went to meet a deadline at last minute demands
Married to having coins always in my pants

I made it to church before it got late
They say it's a good place to get a soul mate
Put my all in a woman like the collection plate
Walked out on the sermon of wedding vows to take

She gave another 'E' for I hurt, feel pain and cry ...

Welcome to E.V.E's Heartbreak

Virginal

Alphonso Taylor

Job Hunt

♍

A broken clock is right twice a day
I've been working so hard on my resume
but, it's short
like a book report
I don't have much experience
Hunting for a salary with benefits
I got my degree
trying to get finances to be free
Training, medical, sick leave, and paid vacations
Trying to stay put in an occupation
My ink pen filling out so many applications
typing up cover letters
sending them through faxers
What can I do
Sick of the saying "Don't call me. I'll call you."
Relaxed and secretly frustrated at an interview
Some managers are unprofessional and they lie
Out to brunch, I could have worn my shirt and tie
They don't want you to earn the pay they make
A job paying ten dollars or more an hour, I'll take
For minimum wage, green paper, I can create
A business card and my palms are never sweaty
A predator that preys on a career for which I'm ready
Fine, I don't mind getting my hands a little dirty
Having to get up in the morning early
Why am I still waiting on a bus
I should be driving a Mercedes with a spare in the trunk
Don't tell me it's the economic slump
My taxes going to war and gas pumps
Okay, what are the positions, a permanent contractor
No matter what, I'm pursuing my goal to be an actor
Stepping up the corporate ladder
You still deny me of a raise or promotion
OOH, I just want to kick all my doors open

Virgo, the Wordmaker

Sign off on the bonus
Shouldn't have to wait so long for a check
Never been convicted, is it because I'm Black
Finding a living on a full time, part time, temporary contract
For a seasonal intern, can I at least be hired
I'm not begging, my own self, I usually fire
Saving up for when I retire
Still, there going to be problems
I'll be stable, but money won't be the problem

Alphonso Taylor

Work for Me

♍

The system will tell you to finish high school and get your diploma. Afterwards, attend college to get a degree. Therefore, you'll be able to find a great job leading into a career. In addition, you'll get full time status and benefits. Without one or two of those certificates, the chances are unlikely.

You graduate from both learning establishments, go into the work field and still can't get a job in your major that you want and deserve to have. Very seldom, you apply in person or go to a job fair. Now, the application process is you send a resume and sometimes along with a cover letter to companies via mail, e-mail, fax and wait for calls. Speaking of calls, some of them get antsy and don't even want you to do that, just to see if you're legit for recruitment. That's why I'm skeptical about giving my date of birth and SSN because it's as if, it's the shady approach to research someone's history without being brought in for questioning. Even putting contact info of previous work places might not always be good because you don't know, if they're giving you a neat reference, whether or not, you left on good terms. I feel my own yearly references are more valuable.

I'll be damned if I go back to school to get a Master's degree, Doctorate, and PhD and you still want to give me an occupation paying barely above minimum wage. Then, there are dropouts who are society's biggest millionaires and billionaires. Most of them are the real crooks and thieves in suits. They get wealthy from poor and middle class people like me. Soon as stocks or source of income goes to a standstill, they're the main ones who'll commit suicide and murder their family.

It seems the jobs that are really hiring are fast food services, janitorial and retail sales to customer services. For most black people, flipping patties and mopping floors might have been the dream job in the early 80s and 90s, but there is so much wanted from us. Since we were denied our freedom, 40 acres, and a mule during Slavery to build the country as we know as America, we had and still have to grind to be more successful entrepreneurs. Through the struggle, it's awful we can't stick together. That's why other minorities such as the Latinos and Hispanics are willing to take the sanitary and food positions because they look out for one another. The Whites of course are going to make their individuals fortunate. Still, all races do harmful things to one another. Retail sales and any hustle to produce revenue are shady especially if it's just commission. The folks in charge only like you when you sell something. If not, then to them you're just a dime a dozen. Teaching is in consideration, but now grade schools to institutes are dangerous. Some are saying, the best way to go is federal governed and that's not guaranteed in layoffs. So, we're artists, specialists, mechanics, doctors, lawyers and more to maintain.

Fabricated ads are run with some jobs saying, they'll start people with 'X' amount of dough. When you get there, they tell you a whole other story and some of us accept it because of the simple fact, we need work. So, you're aboard trying to survive the probation period after being introduced to your staff members, which could be iffy quirks to adjust. Then, that's when all the confusion develops from you passing the test. A manager, he or she and it's often a he decides to have a bad day and starts bickering about you not executing your line of duty when you are. The description was made clear before you applied. Behind closed doors in offices, it's snickering because the supervisor thinks you're frightened of losing your job. The harassment evolves and you're at the boiling point of cussing out someone. Sometimes, you refrain so there won't be any petty excuses of being written up nor have your hours cut. The method is to aim at getting you terminated.

Most of you managers need to get chewed. Some of you think because you have a little bit of power, you talk to folks anyway you want without consequences. It's a reminder to stay professional, but some of y'all have to come off the premise after work hours... Therefore, I don't need you standing over and hounding me with hunched shoulders to make sure I'm performing task. I can work alone and I'll call you, if I need assistance. I don't need you trying to belittle me in front of my co-workers, although some of them are just as worst as you are. You giving me demands? The only thing that gives demands is guts. First of all, you're not paying me the dead presidents I'm really worth with the nickel and diming peanuts. Payroll is sometimes cheesy because checks are coming up short, even with straight deposit. How do you expect some folks to survive when they got children, husbands, wives, bills, car notes, and mortgage, rent and health relations? It's like you don't even care as you're saving your asses from resigning. Most of y'all titles of management, supervision, seniority or whatever is just a sellout and you can get demoted anytime. Your cruelty isn't always justified. Got the nerve to be telling me, if I don't like it, I can find another profession. Good because the last time I documented it, I'm the CEO of my own destiny, not you. Everybody wants to be chief and not enough Indians...

I'm tired of taking odd gigs. I can't really see myself progressing at a company because of the filthy pettiness. I want to be a HNIC and build my empire and entourage and expand like the mobsters to mafia. Just go in cooperation

Virgo, the Wordmaker

for myself so I can say, I work for me and hire my upstanding citizens. Soon, I'll be able to say, *you work for me*.

Alphonso Taylor

Waitlist

♍

I'm just bait dangling in the mist
Wading in the water tryna catch a good fish
but, I usually get dissed
Lady or ladies
Am I not your type
Does my name and number
have to look like The Price Is Right
I don't showcase any games
I show high interest rates
with a little bank and no driver's slate
All I have is me
You still put me on a waitlist
Give me a reason
because for unconditional love I'm feenin'
I think with me its bacteria
With another man, it's a banquet
A lot of chicks say I must have my shit together
Some of you don't have it down pat internally
BAGGAGE, EXCUSES, ISSUES
DAMN, for myself, I shall have a box of tissue
A few didn't know what it's like to be treated right
To have a real date with light
 Get good loving at the end of a night
DON'T SLEEP ON LITTLE MEN
Got power bigger than multiples of ten
The first time I confessed I was in love
was after the first time I got dumped
I'm nowhere near garbage
I'm just a young man who acts like a grumpy man
of Cream of Wheat feelings
I shouldn't even respect women
No, I'm just kidding
Expect from me and I try
Expect from you, you tell me to wait

Virgo, the Wordmaker

Then, when I wanna move on...

WAIT!

Alphonso Taylor

Tug of Women: Younger - Alphonso - Older

my

Officially, I entered the dating world at the age of eighteen. In other words, have my first, real girlfriend. I was just gathering the basis of how to start and at least finish a date, regardless if it was dinner, movies etc. I really didn't have an age preference at that time, except I grew to like beautiful big women and receiving young attractions. Due to the numerous amounts of rejections I have had, I even settled for mediocrity.

When I became a legal, adult male, I went through an unusual turning point. I started to get sick of women around my age and a tad bit older. I felt they're always too picky and full of games. The understanding of what we both were looking for wasn't exact matches. Well, at least I tried to make sense of my ambitions and morals in a relationship.

Eventually, I started being attracted to older women. For a while, it seemed so weird and maybe it still is, but I can't help what I like. I chose these alternatives because, I once believed some older women are straightforward. They know what they really want and are done lollygagging in the fields, at least some of them. I don't look to be taught anything. I just see what I can offer to the experience.

The common factor, I always face with women I come across in my life is, the majority of them has baggage and self-conscious issues. It's as if, the damage has already been done, when I'm the runner up. Sometimes, I don't mind the sob stories because; I have had a fair share of insecurities and bad results from a male's perspective. So every now

Virgo, the Wordmaker

and then, I can relate, which leads to me showing effeminacy. I have expressed deepest and closest secrets to scars of my past. Growing up, I didn't really see many examples of how an organized relationship should be. I'm as emotional and sensitive as the opposite gender of me and I'm not soft or a bitch. I can't quite comprehend, why a lot of women say, I don't listen or pay attention. Some of you just like to hear yourselves flap your gums at me, like I'm still moist on the lobes. I think it's reversed. **Y'ALL DON'T PAY ATTENTION OR LISTEN TO ME.** Just because I can't recite word for word everything you tell me, doesn't mean it's not programmed in memory. Then, when I summarize the information, you're looking shocked. I try hard to feel for a woman to let her know, there is a man like myself who cares and don't want to be on the roster as another asshole. Until this day, if any woman has given me the title, I'll swallow my rage to reputation and wear it. I can't be the "good-guy gem" all the time to women especially those who didn't really deserve it in the first place. I often have the objective to be the knight in shining armor, not the hero/saver.

Later on, high expectations, bleak maintenance, and standards were expected of me. Usually, I don't mind going all out to meet them. Just being that supporter, comforter and more to see to it a woman remains glamorous for duration. I do this with compliments, gifts, and extras to show how romantic I can be with my natural sense of humor. The gist is, sometimes I be struggling on the verge of going penniless to keep her pleased. Not to have bragging rights, but I feel I do better than some men with a six-figure stipend.

I'll take this moment to close my eyes, so I can inhale and EXHALE ... Now, I'm about to go cold ballistic. Finally, I want to nip it in the bud. I don't know when it will be the last lash out. Feel me! PLEASE, FEEL ME!

The mess that has been driving me crazy is, when a

woman asks or tells me to do something ... Jump! I suppose to be like, *how high?* Move *pronto,* Alphonso! My responses must be, "Sure, sweetie!", "Not a problem, honey.", "Okay, baby!" Then, when I look forward to her doing her part, I get attitude, backtalk, delays, and a hard time in return. It feels with a drop of a hat, I'm put on the backburner. I wonder what's the problem and why do I have to be on some waiting period?

I have had a lady say to me, *"I do things, when I feel like doing them."* Me personally, I DON'T WANNA HEAR THAT SHIT! Tell it to the preacher! Suppose I say, "I'll treat you like a queen, when I feel like it?" I'm willing to give you the shirt off my torso and it's not like, I really do it to get any reciprocation. It's just the principle; I have feelings, needs and want too. In other words, my cake and eat it. I'm not looking for a superwoman or requesting much variety. All I'm saying is, once in a blue moon or windy evening; can I be catered to without any suggestions? I exercise patience, but sometimes I want things like yesterday. Shouldn't have to be postponed until a couple of days, weeks and months as you put me front and center on cue. We're both into writing and you don't have to acknowledge me for editing ¾ of your novel in stance. Now, if you give me a copy, I'm tossing it in the trash.

As a few women decide to come through for me, they say, I'm using them. How in the hell am I using you? You gained from the shed of my blood, sweat, tears, and financial earnings. Constantly, smiling in my face and acting prissy. Then when everything isn't peaches and cream, you have the belief, I'm ruined for life. Your doubtfulness of me is so severe and still you search for me to make you my wife.

I've been given the explanation that there's no 50/50 in a relationship. I feel, if a man and a woman is not about making each other happy or intensifying the happiness already

Virgo, the Wordmaker

available, what's the purpose of staying together? Now, I see why most of us, including myself are single. I'm a strong believer of fairness. If we're down, we pick each other up.

When it comes to sex, I'm not the highly sexed sign in the universe. But *ooooh*, I possess multi-dimensions of freakiness, which I can get wild and nasty. My affection is artfully deep of a sensitive lover from cuddling, foreplay to coitus. I focus on minutiae to make sure BOTH of our anatomy has orgasmic relief. I would do it from a strand of a woman's hair to the tip of her toenails. Whatever is started between the sheets, a Virgo finishes it.

Lately, I've been hearing the strangest remarks. Some women said, I done left them hanging, they haven't climaxed from me in a while, and I only seem to be out for myself. I can't see how that is, when I'm always the move maker to the most idealistic and creative one in the bedroom to adventurous somewhere else. In other words, I stay putting in the effort to allure fantasies to fulfillment. Why the process of Bump-N-Grind has to begin with me often? I even have to tell a woman to take her clothes off or I do all the undressing, so we can get busy. **SHIT, UNDRESS AND SPOIL ME!** If my drive hasn't been functioning properly and it's in a recession like the past horrible economy, then so be it. All the time, my mind is saying, "*Yessss!*" and now sometimes my body says, "*No!*" Some of it has to do with excessive masturbating I have done, which is not always suitable. Then, again I mind as well be with L*apalm*a. Meanwhile, I don't have to read any stories or do a damn tape to prove my sexuality. Right now, I deserve to hibernate. I'm sick of doing the seducing and not be appreciated. Honestly, I think some of you women can't keep up as I'm in my prime. I know one thing. For now on, when an opportunity develops, I'm going to the extreme of Erotica and if a woman isn't for it, SHAME ON YOU because I'm on fire. It's no shame in my flame and I don't like to hold back. How dare y'all to judge or question my sex appeal, when some of you probe as deadbeats with inhibitions. Who are you to insult my *insexilligence?*

The virgin in me, *she* wants to know, do I turn you on, making you wet? Do you desire me as much as I desire you? I don't ever want a woman to feel obligated to have sex with me, just because I want to. Definitely, I'm not a hard guy to please. I like for the moves to be made on me for a change. Catch me off guard with the sensual surprises and I will surrender. As usual, a woman does the ordeal to me as indication, it's only a one time, sultry treat and that's it. Basically teasing me, knowing I will crave for more. In the future, if any woman feels I'm worth a once of happenings, we shall be a one night stand, if she don't see me as value for various thrills and privileges.

It's a saying, I think too much with my dick. Well, why not …? Practically, I live a quiet life. I don't hang out or party a lot. No drugs or alcohol. I'm in my own fast lane, going rampant and gutter to gradually come to a halt, since I don't truly have anybody. When I care about that aspect, it backfires and it's snotty. Daily, I'm on a mission with my grind, hustling to creep on my come up. A lot of you ladies don't understand that because when a man is trying to be successful, you think he's competing with you and preventing you from reaching your goals. Firstly my dick stays erect because I have to fuck haters, low-lives, and those who are already on top trying to screw me. They do this so I won't make it to where they're at. Secondly, I got a hard-on, so I won't have to bring any stress to the household from dealings of society. I just want to have a delicious, home cook meal, hobbies/activities, bomb ass *hanky-panky*, and relax in my lady's arms. So yeah, 24/7 I keeps a fat pointy, stiff one, when necessary.

Virgo, the Wordmaker

At last, but never least, it has been broken down to me that I like older women the most and I just be with younger women to get them pregnant. THAT'S THE MOST RIDICULOUS CRAP, I EVER HEARD IN MY LIFE. I am with a woman, which we may have similar interest in things to further explore our chemistry and compatibility. As far as I'm concerned, almost any woman can have my kids, if it's really meant to be. If my fertilizer and her soil are healthy enough to plant seeds, it will be a blessing after a strong discussion of parenthood and that's what we want. Hopefully, I can be already established and a husband. Don't want to be a baby daddy and cursed with miscarriages. For real, I'm letting nature take me wherever it wants to go as long as it's positive. I don't have say so anymore. I'll just be a drifter. **WHATEVER HAPPENS HAPPENS!** Finally, I got it solved with the younger and older SAGA. Check it out!

Young women, most of you come from negligence of your daddies, abuse, rape, or mistreatment of men. Those key elements will make it a battle for any man to be the appropriate partner, spouse etc. Therefore; you want me to baby you. The last time I checked, we're consenting adults. Your hand, I'm not gonna always hold. By myself, I can't steer the whole load. Too many times, I've been down that road. So, if you're not ready for something new, CHANGE, a different level and the best of both worlds, YOU CAN GETTA STEPPIN'! I will no longer do chases or any begging. I've learned my lesson. I'm about 1+1=2, a unit, team and just me and you. You're not greater than me and your so called independence doesn't scare me away. I'm there to help like you did me and be by side, not pushed astray and left in disarray. Made me pretend I was something; I'm not, up to this day. To you, I was deadly attracted. You took it for granted and I got distracted… I won't dial you any more after midnight. I won't be going to your house so we could make love at the crack of daylight. You can delete me all you want from your MySpace page and change it to private. I'll still do me and be the modest. You don't have to put no more songs on my iPod or view for me my e-mails. In technology, I will prevail. You said if we were so bad to each other, howcome we haven't found anybody else? I can't take the drama no more and I'm focused on myself. I know I made decisions and did things that were naïve. I know I caused confusion flaring pet-peeves. With me, you can continue to not be a diva and see the hue, red. I *ushered my confessions of cheating and won't have insomnia in my bed. With another guy, you can stay stuck on having a ride. It's more to that I want to invest in and confide. We don't have to have what normal, engaged couples should have. A roof over head as a place we call home, crib or pad. Now I think back, that's was the only time I really seen you jolly, when I had a vehicle almost the size of a dolly. No wonder, you had liked to keep staring at me, while I was driving. You was probably saying, "Yeah, I got this man to get a set of wheels and I'm not gonna do anything we planned."* **CONNIVING!** If we really wanted to share and step out of monogamy, we could have talked about it decently and not act like we didn't want to be here. I mean honestly, discipline me if there's an error of me saying and wanted to be with you for a lifetime. Does it whistle and fade like bell chimes? Although you said we were friends, family and I'll make a good dad, you don't have to feel like being the carrier of my unborn offspring. We were done, so I packed your things and got back my ring. The rollercoaster kept bouncing. Damn, if you were gonna be Mrs. Taylor, we couldn't even make it to counseling. I was devastated and all it can ever do is making me stronger. Oh by the way, **TELL EVERYONE YOU KNOW I DON'T LOVE YOU ANY LONGER.** I thought the lease was I'm glued to you forever? *It is what it is.* Don't know what the future holds, I don't go backwards and it's a wrap, which is clever. Told you, you resented me. Abruptly, we ended on a 3 to 3.

Older women, the majority of you are from the matching incidents of torture. You're the former generation. You like to pimp (play) me to see how far you can carry it. You always try to hold out, while I do all the putting out. I ask you with caution from the beginning, how you feel about us, instead of being tricky. But oh no, some of y'all are so set beyond in your own ways, thinking you're gonna control me and the situation, simply...? I don't care if you been around the *block* more than I have or gone where I'm going. It doesn't give you the fortitude to use my **EMOTIONS** for toying. Yeah, you may have children near, above or exactly my age. Still, I'm smart over my years, known as the sage. I'm not about games and without feelings getting involved; I can have adult fun. It's a certain crush I might have felt, before the amusement had begun. In the long run, you could be, but YOU'RE NOT MY MOTHER AND I'M NOT YOUR SON. For any woman who has a grown one, if I and he were to fight, I would see everything to it that I would have won. And I know damn well I'm mature enough to change an older woman's mind. It's that number barrier and I'm looked at as, *who's this whippersnapper to dictate how things gonna unwind?* I was in your room about 5 times and at the same time, you're not gonna rule me and lead me on to bruise my ego. If my flirtatious aggression is too much for you to handle, just say so. I swear I won't even bother you anymore. For sure, I can leave alone and ignore. It's nice you fooled me once, maybe twice. You'll never fool me **THRICE.** Spare me the celibate details because it isn't nothing I'm missing and if you didn't have any intentions of giving me the golden, seasoned gumbo, **I KNOW IT ISN'T NOTHING I'M MISSING.** I'll take it for whatever it was, teasing, sighs, feeling, hugging, and kissing. Y'all rather give me purple balls and what do I be doing to get the hostile, female intuition?

I don't have a preference or ideal description no more. It's the same shit, different woman, regardless of era. Arguments, warnings, idle threats, disagreements, disrespect, bad name calling, miscommunication, mood swings, mental troubleshooting, conflict of interest, headaches, HEARTBREAKS and the list goes on. Nothing is ever right. It's got to be something wrong. This plight has been happening for too long. I've become bittersweet and drastic. Now, it'll be difficult for me to put all my grass in one basket. You say you like me. You say you love and you're in love with me, except it arrives with restraints. Overall, I'm exhausted with the whining, bitchiness and complaints. I debate; do I be early or late for these connections to almost turn into an affair of hate? You say you want a NICE man and you're tired of the men who are dealers, criminals and bad boys, **SLAPPING YOUR ASS AROUND**. Soon as you have the good man, **YOU SEE HIM AS A SUCKER, SHIT ON HIM, AND TRY TO BRING HIM DOWN**. Damn if you do or damn if you don't have him. You say your body becomes steel, when cruel dude is **STRAPPING YOU AND TAKING YOUR COOCHIE LOFT.** Then, if I'm on top to be the good penis in your life like you wanted, you tell me my little muscles wouldn't matter and if you want, you can get me off. The cowards get away with murder and its morbid a grown man like me gets the shambles. One **WENCH**, your ex-boyfriend was a hustler and exploited you for your money. I took you in and tried to show you that vinegar is not sweeter than honey, since you think DC men act so funny. There were symptoms; you could have been having my

Virgo, the Wordmaker

child. I don't know why my possibilities seem so mild. Then, you pulled the ultimate betrayal, a week after Valentine's Day with that hotel stunt. You gonna do me foul because I don't smoke blunts? You wrote me two poems called, *'Open'* and *'Trust'*. It wasn't meant to be for I don't do *angel dust*? You can keep it moving for good and go suck the devil's nuts. I've seen many situations that were sly. I never thought in order for a woman to be with me, she had to get high. *Arggggh,* I stormed out in the cold all alone to help the remedy in me drown as I was roaming in town. Distress took its course causing me to wheeze and frown. I can't even get closure. There are so many risks of deceit and viruses that can lead to my discomposure. I don't put it past that the Nice Guy theory is accurate. MOST OF US DO FINISH LAST. **FUCK ME** because I won't keep being the one and from these soap operas, I will flabbergast. I am looking forward to Aphrodite and Venuses. All I get is Medusas and actual Madeas. They say, beside every good man is a good woman and I haven't yet of that contained. I'm thinking I have companionship, its pain. E.V.E is so hurt, *she's* medieval in vain. *She* be saying Alphonso, Virgo baby, this shit is crazy. *Yep, yep, yep, yep, yep, yep!* Just let them all be and concentrate on you. What have you done for **YOU** lately? Stay in motion with your *pep, pep, pep, pep, pep, pep!*

When it's a final separation, a lot of females like to throw rocks at me of how they were such a good woman to me, like I didn't donate the **COURTESY** of my manhood. I forgot though, that what I do is forgettable. For most of y'all, I would have amputated my right elbow and *DIIIIE*. I would have kissed and drunk the tears from your eye. Probably, if I was to pull a Chris Brown to Rihanna or a little rough looking and taller with offers on a silver platter, I could be taken serious. Then, it won't be very delirious. You steady categorizing me of a shortcoming. From me, you're running.

My loyalty to you, you're not ready for and you avoid. I don't know the reasons with me you're so paranoid. You seem prepared and you're never scared though, when I'm doing to benefit you. Then, when I talk about me or us, it's a fuss. If you don't give a fuck, THEN I DON'T GIVE A FUCK. TOUGH LUCK! It seems you get a kick out of putting me in dilemmas, like I suppose to be desperate, **WHEN I'M NOT**. And for the record, fuck the whole internet, chat room and online hook up shit. I've LEARNED and realize it's not up to par and most of you chicks live too far. My phalanges don't wanna be in that type of cookie jar. I'm better with meeting in person from the start. A prophecy has been foretold to me; my lady to be is somewhere long distant and quite passes me... Because I'm worn out, I'll escort myself in a drought house with ease. It was taught to me, I can't keep being the rat to fall for y'all cheese. THE BLIND LEADING THE BLIND!

I'm not a saint, but I'm wretched with being taken through the changes and blues. I have a migraine trying to draw clues. I think my legacy might be of one of my inspirations, Langston Hughes. Didn't really get involved with any women, didn't get married or father any children. He just made an impact in the world as a great poet, novelist and journalist. To me, that's the best accomplishment any man could have, especially for a man like me. I got almost everything in this life figured out. It seems I'll never know what this "man and a woman union" is all about. My forefathers continue to inform me that I'll be okay and I'll find my way. Most ladies are complicated creatures and *HEARTLESS*. Also, they tell me that some women, you should be lucky a man like me put his frustrations on paper. Most men aren't in control of their agony, will hurt you physically or worse, and then gather you in the afterlife, *LATER*. It's one lady I'm stalking and her name is, Success with a big ass, pretty *green* dress. **WAIT TILL I GET IT RIGHT…!** She's my primary soul mate.

   The tragic comedy lives on. I don't know when I'll be able to laugh about this, although it's kidding me. ***Oh, Ha, Ha, Ha!*** I get it now. ***LOL!*** It's been a good one. The satire is on me. Silly me. **SILLY ME!** Well, it's the end and I won't even mention the outcome, unless it's brought to me. **I CAN'T HAVE OR SATISFY THEM ALL**. Specifically, I'm emotionally tired of taking the losses. In general, **IT'S NEVER MY LOSS**. It feels like a waste of T.I.M.E (Trust, Intimacy, Money and Energy). The trust and intimacy looks gone forever. Money and energy are newly replaceable in search for that surreal fairytale, if it's not extinct and even if it's just common law.

Alphonso Taylor

Virgo and a Woman

♍

It was instant attraction
Best approach I've ever made to a woman of my satisfaction
When we met, I didn't have a personality
She showed me the essence of fun in this harsh reality
The first woman to truly make me happy
Always having me to keep a balanced chi
Giving me the peace I need without any stress
Made me feel welcomed as my heart she caressed
The way she spoke made our conversations intellectual
Raising my curiosity about her being sexual
Didn't rush anything, but I quickly fell in love
The vibe of each other just made us budge
My life from the Sirens and lamia she saved
while having precious dreams about being a mermaid
A woman of culture who has real sense
A divine example of womanhood to my expense
I swear no men can have her
I'll make their lives natural disasters
Yes, we're going to have our troubles
Thick and thin to strive and be humbled
Accepted me for my imperfections
We can have intercourse without any affection
If possible, give birth through Immaculate Conception
Symbolic like the Virgin Mary
She's the woman; a Virgo was dying to marry

Virgo, the Wordmaker

Leave My Beauty Alone

♍

I never really look at it as being on the prowl or in the market. I see it as true essence, I like to pursue, if it's worthwhile. To get through the infatuation stage, my mind must be occupied. I like to get acquainted with the personality more, instead of the physique. Once I know a little of the inside, then the beauty is emancipated. Its treasure I discovered and at least earned to have for myself.

As soon as I'm always close or I got the woman, all of a sudden, these guys come from nowhere and try to take her. They don't even vouch for the lady until I and she are seen together. They feel so much, they can do better than I can and are more qualified for the job. And it goes that way because us men, we're the workers and the female is the employer. When we holler, it's an interview and she'll give the final approval of whether or not, our skills are enough to hire for dating. The only difference is SOME of us have to bring our own money to the table. If we do things correct, it can become an advance for a serious relationship, to get the booty and more. What kills me is, if I'm already in the position, why does fellows cock block me?

If I'm not with my other half or lady of interest, there be dudes who'll literally come to her, asking and saying things like, *"You still with that little, bitch ass nigga? Why you with him? You need to leave and be with a real cat."* What's sad, these chumps barely know me and make assumptions that I'm not treating her right and they're the chosen ones to do so.

Is it because, I'm a well educated, made man and connected, while y'all game seems infected? Is it my confidence with **ZIGZAGGING** swagger, which of my craft, I'm a great master? Man, I never have been the envious type. If a chick feels you're cuter, richer and the mighty contender to sweep her off her feet, I'll step aside. That way, the comparison and contrast won't be too much of a mystery to solve. Let the best man win. I don't play, *Whose Dick Is Bigger?* She wasn't for me and I go on knowing I'll get in where I belong.

Another man and I after the same woman is a catastrophe waiting to happen. If she hasn't yet giving either one of us the time of day, I don't know why he got beef with me. Don't be mean-mugging me! **I AIN'T THE PROBLEM.** Are we really supposed to brawl over a broad? Although that's not something that usually comes between two men, I see a few men I used to be cool with will slit your throat for a shot of pussy. Then, the woman is laughing at both of us because she thinks we're wrapped on her finger and I'm not. When lines, trains and traffic are developed, I don't do those.

Find your own main squeeze! Hypothetically, its ashamed most of you men would do anything slick for seconds to leftovers. All the beauty worldwide and a man rather take someone else's. Even the *King of Pop* said, "The Girl Is Mine." Sometimes, I feel like with any man, I'm Popeye tangling with Bluto for an Olive Oyl.

Actually, these men are compensated. I can't seem to exist with a beauty for a very long time, so she's up for grabs, no matter how I try to make it work. It's as if, never had her and I failed. Wishes are made for a split up and they are granted. It could be a friendship or a commitment of romance and it's as if, I can never see departure cementing, unless it just dawn on me as it goes downhill.

Virgo, the Wordmaker

Phat Women

♍

DAMN, I like fat women
I mean its so much cushion
Bodies as big as a house
I like to lay on them like a bed or couch
Smother my face in their titties as pillows
Have all that jelly jiggle
Don't have to think or tell me twice
I've never been intimidated
Bring me the bones that's overweight
A beautiful sight to see when they're naked
Wrap me up like a blanket
Baby, you can't break me or hurt me
I'll step to you personally like I'm Hercules
Once I went fat
I'd never gone back
It's like going from a cheeseburger to a Big Mac
a French fry to a chicken thigh
a pan to a pot
from a street to a wide ass parking lot
Big girls, a lot of fellas can't stand
I'm glad I chose otherwise and got with the program
If I ever become a rapper
I would change the history of music videos
by having phat dimes for all purposes
I would change B-E-T to F-E-T
There should be fine thick females in JET Beauty of the Week
I thank Hollywood for Mo'nique
I have nothing against ladies whom are skinny
The men whom missing out
For me there's plenty of phat women, DAMN

Alphonso Taylor

Perfectionist: The Physical World

♍

The majority of people around the world are not satisfied with the physical appearance of their bodies. Most people are born with a disability in which, they are usually ostracized in life. This can happen from birth to full adulthood. Often, they are not accepted as a human being to others. That's why most disabled people fight for a cure or surgery to be well formed like other people.

During adolescence, many teenagers experience acne. They feel as though their faces are not clear as their friends or other people. When many people break out on their face, they'll bust or pick with the pimples, so it will not be noticeable especially in public. Some people buy cosmetics from drug stores for acne. If it gets worst, they recommend a dermatologist. Everyone wants an attractive image, even if it's just their face.

As girls get older developing into women, they start wearing makeup to feel beautiful. They get accustom to foundation on a daily routine. Also, some women add extra hair, known as tracks to their natural hair to make it longer and stylish. For women's body, most of them get plastic surgery for their breasts and butt to look sexier and for sexual pleasure. Every now and then, women shave certain areas of their bodies for sexual pleasure as well. Many men do not want a woman without a petite shape of her body. In other words, women are more attractive by the thickness of certain areas of their figures.

Most men lift weights/work out to feel comfortable about themselves toward women. Some women like men with big biceps and triceps throughout their bodies. Men usually don't change appearance of themselves, but a clean trim, equivocally a haircut. Once in a while, a man would make an extraordinary change. Now, a lot of men take drugs to enlarge their penis and length of time of erection for sexual pleasure. Today in society, many women feel good sex is equated to, if a man has a particular penis size. That's not even fully legit anymore because it's all about a man knowing how to use and what to do with it.

Universally, the population of some humans is ecstatic with their skin color. Still, most like to get a tan to be the same skin color as another race. In other words, some people want to be White, Black, Indian, Chinese etc. They will even go as far as flesh bleaching. On numerous occasions, folks are getting piercing and tattoos as a form of fashion. It is not always about the appearance of people that makes them want to change a proportion of their bodies, but they might just have personal situations in their lives.

All humans should be satisfied with the natural image of themselves. It shall be about whom you are, not your looks. The world is lost in who looks fine, pretty, sexy, cute, handsome, fat, and ugly. People are worried about how they will look as they get older especially, when they reach their forties, fifties, sixties, and seventies. If the Creator wanted us to be a certain figure, then it would have happened before we were born the way we are now.

Emotional

Alphonso Taylor

Seductive Temperature

ny

Feeling sentimental, its thunderous desire I stare into your eyes
My touch crawls all over your polished-smooth thighs
Between them, the weather is a hundred degrees
Misty and raining from the grip of our warm hug
I know we're about to make some passionate love
I've been patiently waiting for this special treat
Finally, our organs in no space or time meet
The moment is right as we exchange a deep sweet kiss
Shedding skin like snakes, we hiss
Slowly, you taste and jerk the magic stick
Then all of a sudden
soothing your soft neck
 I make your nipples as hard as pushbuttons
outlining every spot down to your stomach
Your pretty toes begin to curl
as I gently spit shine your diamond pearl
Then ease my sex finger in and out your ring
My moaning be the tune as you scream and sing
HARDER, DEEPER, I just take my time
It's yours and its mine
I like to draw back and see myself inside
your tight beautiful puddle of slick water as I slip and slide
In the middle of each stroke
our bodies get real soaked
scratching the color of seduction in each other's flesh
You want to be in control
Get on top and ride any way you like
Changing positions, I bump and grind
for a long time the wide ass juicy behind
Simultaneously, we're loud, shaking and reaching climax
Tears fall as a light drizzle
Your muscles squeeze me and throb like heartbeats of pleasure
Losing my breath, I release clouds into the night

Virgo, the Wordmaker

Don't surface the full moon
Talking and cuddling as we get some rest feeling lovely
The sun will be up soon

Alphonso Taylor

Afterglow

♍

Discreet low
Sweet low
Discreet aftergloooow
CUMMING forth to carry me home
I called on Hermes and what did I see
CUMMING forth to carry me home

Giiiiirl, your sex I wanna **RAVISH**
My planet's humming **LAVISH**
A great **KISSER**
Love **HISSER**
Sugar **SIZZLER**
Peck lips like **TWIZZLERS**
Ecstasy, I'll take you to the **EXTREME**
Unveil fragrance of au naturel **CRÈME**
Senses to the occasion are **WISE**
Horny, Mellow on the **RISE**

Compromise, flow, this time we take it slow
As our breathing together blends in the afterglow

Feel the heat as my face is pressed against your cheek
More attentive reproduction, I can't hide and seek

From last night, let's complete what we started
I lie on you between cozy legs parted

When I suck your breasts, I mold your estrus
Bring out the nymph of you in cunnilingus

Virgo, the Wordmaker

Stay with me, please don't leave, don't say no
You like how I work this solo, chill with a Virgo

If you see me tremble, it's not because I'm nervous
I'm overwhelmed with zeal, OHH you're so fucking gorgeous

Am I dreaming, sexing your fine ass
A goddess sculpted with class and sass

Ms. Mooommy, Moooommy, I cry mi **AMOUR**

Make you cum many times, times **FOUR**

Freaky **ROOTS**

Knockin' **BOOTS**

The owl in me **HOOTS**

OOOH, OOOH, your aqua all over me **SHOOTS**

Is it still possible to **BREATHE**

Sweat on one another, we **WREATHE**

I can't resist your **PRESENCE**

You got me sprung of this **INDULGENCE**

Baby, forget our signs, while we both intertwine
Put that tingle in your spine and have you float on Spica 9

You're all mine, don't ever wanna be rushed
E.V.Enly, my body to you remains flushed

Skin slapping sounds to the bottom of each pound
My mushroom thrusts the tunnel of your swell mound

We're close to explosion as you give us the notion
I'm ready to pour lotion to mix it in with potion

Bass and soprano in unison hit a chord
We can't hold it in and we yell out, OH LORD, LORD, LORD

Sweet loooow

Alphonso Taylor

Afterglooow

CUMMING forth to carry me home, home, hoooome

Virgo, the Wordmaker

Food Poem

♍

Hmmm, **I enjoys me some food**
like the hunger for booty when I'm in the mood
Eating it to get back my groove
As if, I met a chick named Felecia
Slicing through her *Cheese Pizza*

Oops, **my bad, this is a food poem**
So rich and warm as *Butter Popcorn*
For a snack, I want a *Peanut-butter* **and** *Jelly Sandwich*
Maybe *Sloppy Joes* **from** ***Manwich***
Ham, *Breasts* **of a** *Turkey* **and** *Chicken*
Collard Greens, Yams, **Wow, its Thanksgiving**
Cranberry, Biscuits, **and those funky** *Chitterlings*
In almost every *Salad,* **I can see Christmas**
It's the *Pecan, Apple,* **and** *Sweet Potato Pie*
I mess with *Bagels*, **but not that** *Bread* **called** *Rye*
Toast, Waffles, Cereal, **scrambled** *Eggs, Sausage*
Pancakes, Bacon, Scrapple, Oatmeal, Grits
English Muffins, Hash Browns, **and** *Omelets*
Any time of day, I can have breakfast

Sometimes it feels I can be my own server
Hotdogs, Chips, Onion Rings, **delicious** *Burgers*
Cookies, Cake, Ice-cream **and I don't do** *Yogurt*
Don't think I'm choosy when it comes to dessert
Pickles, Honey buns, Peanuts, **and glazed** *Doughnuts*
Candy **contribute to this thing known as junk**

My health can be more eligible
Consuming fruit and vegetables
Tomatoes, Onions, Lettuce, and Cabbage
Bananas, Raisins, Apples, Pears, and Oranges
Peas, Spinach and Broccoli **keeps everything green**

Alphonso Taylor

Corn **and** *Carrots* **to excellent hygiene**
I make sure I gain carbohydrates and protein

I wanna go scuba diving for some *Tuna Fish*
Seafood at its best with roasted *Shrimp*
I never got full from eating *Crabs*
I like cocktail sauce with *Salmon* **and raw** *Clams*
No *Lobster* **yet, but I have had greasy** *Duck*
No *Shark Meat*, *Turtle Soup* **and I ate** *Scallops*
Calamari Crayfish, **I'm not a stranger to** *Squid*

Ocean food ain't scary, if you don't see eyelids
I can travel the world with a *Steak* **from Philly**
Pasta, Lasagna, **and** *Spaghetti* **to Italy**
Give me those *Plantains* **from Jamaica**
That spicy *Rice* **from Thailand and Sri Lanka**
Shorba **in Algeria, a country in Africa**
Burritos, Fajitas, Quesadillas **at Mexico**
Tacos **to** *Nachos*, **everywhere its New Mexico**
Empanadas **on the coast of Puerto Rico**
Kimchi **comes in a tradition that's Korean**
I like *Swetish Meatballs* **from Sweden**
Mangu, **a great dish that's Caribbean**
Have to change menu of recipes every other week
Souvlaki **in Greece is so Greek**
Sushi **in Japan is so Japanese**
Beef Lo Mein **in China is so Chinese**

I must be alert of high cholesterol and clogged arteries
Heart attacks to diseases and diabetes
Salmonella poison, trichinosis and cancer
Eating habits, the pyramid don't have all the answers
I eat on a modernly basis
These food chains to reactions can be a riot
I try my best to maintain a nutritious diet

Virgo, the Wordmaker

Old Man Genre

♍

Yeah, everyone hits it on the nose
I'm old-fashioned
From everything I do to dancing
The Stone Age type
I should be watching movies in black and white
A latest O.G
Young mind in charge still using chivalry
My third leg ain't limping with a cane
Have a good memory for a brain
Back-in-the-day-stuff, I know names
My peers and elders be amazed by my knowledge
That this wrinkled piece of writing will be a sonnet
I keep folks intrigued because my genre is so unique
Its gonna be around for a long time like antiques

Alphonso Taylor

Born First

♍

I could have been aborted
But, I was supported
by a man who is not biological

After him, he named me
Claimed me
Halfway raised me

I remember
It was the fifth September
My birthday gift was my sister

Am I the oldest by initiation
Was I forced to lead the way
Setting examples as the first and only son

Thank God, I look like my mother
I never knew my real father
By blood, I don't have a brother

I had to be the protector
Man of the households
Until I became an independent provider

Childhood to manhood
Mistakes and sacrifices I made, misunderstood
Only two children, I still turned out good

Virgo, the Wordmaker

Spirits in My Sleep

♍

Can I sleep like a baby
Without my dreams being so shady
I'm dead sleepy with my vision burning
My covers strap me down from tossing and turning
I'm kicking and screaming
What the hell am I dreaming
Flipping my pillows because they're wet from sweat
Something wants to take over my bed with malicious threats
Regardless, if it's made up
In shock, I have to wake up
Spirits appear in forms of dark shadows
Invading the small area in my room with stirs of echoes
I'll kill them off, if I snore
As they melt into the floor
Then I have to stay up for a while
to calm myself like a startled child
They vanish giving me warnings
I feel safe, when I rise in the morning

Alphonso Taylor

Redemption

♍

Redemption in the spreading of wings
to cleanse unrighteousness and redeem
Soar high with the Creator
Everlasting life in Paradise
overseeing a world full of grief and sunshine
A sinner commits a sacrilege
There are conflicts in revelations
Abide by the scriptures
Fly through the graves
Cast forgiveness before the black hole
to pass away, be saved and judged
Some beliefs are its no heaven or hell
We see what we could have been, but failed
Then we're supposed to suffer forever
Where we go from here is a religious tangle
For some of us to emerge from mortals as angels

Virgo, the Wordmaker

Tears of Triumph

♍

Centering myself away from colors of contention
No longer will my spirit be hitched, my dreams will become non-fiction
I will count blessings, no luck
I have access to open all gates to my future, without leaving one shut
I want to conquer missions on the first attempt
May not always have a second opportunity to use the energy sent to me from Power I can't see

My structure is to upgrade many lost generations
With forces of serenity and care, I'll build a foundation
Because of downfalls I've encountered, opinions believe I'm not worth enough
I weaned through the hardest waves
Swam through milky swamps
Fought forlorn fog
Christened cries for deceased temples
I didn't have a chance to say goodbye
I'm still elevating and unstoppable
No one or anything can't destroy me, but the Creator
My will as a lone wolf stands way too strong
You can see determination burn in my eyes
Filled with H20 to evaporate across the skies
I'm the brave one, seething to be released
To dominate the crisis of watching my back every time I step into the streets

Alphonso Taylor

Not be stressed about being robbed, kidnapped, shot, **stabbed, or killed**
I'm thrilled to dominate terrible predictions; I'll never succeed, so in my aura they can't proceed

Adversaries want to get on my nerves
Provoke me to attack
I have voices tell me not to strike
Wisdom have demolished them before I could even blink
I'm a one-warrior regime
I've been juggling to be supreme

Vengeful to hold my titles
Relentless to avoid turmoil
Combative to be the remaining heir of my throne
Hopefully, when it's time to relax for good, I can just go home
Lord, please take me home
Eternally, my triumph will weep
My last tears washed away my last fears in these last past years
I will not live according to judgments cast at me about my birthplace, education, physical images, financial status, living condition, ethnicity or religion
I was born by myself and can only be myself
A child, lamb and servant of God

Alphonso Taylor

E.V.E's Glossary

♍

Effeminate – sensitive just like a female

Virginal – belief of still young and fresh with a whole lot to give

Emotional – hurt, feel pain and cry

Hermes – the messenger of gods, Roman deity to Mercury

Spica – brightest star in the constellation of the Virgo

Alphonso Taylor

About the Author

Alphonso "Al" Taylor was born and bred in Southeast, Washington DC. He is a graduate of Duke Ellington School of Performing Arts. Also, he's an alumni from the University of the District of Columbia with a BA in Theatre Arts. Aside from writing, Alphonso enjoys acting, which he performed in many theatrical productions in the DC area. He released his first book of poetry, *Bible of an Owl: A Collection of Poems* in 2006. On the follow-up, he released the sequel, his second book, *Bible of an Alligator: A Collection of Poems* in 2007. In 2008, Alphonso Taylor portrayed his much softer side and erotic debut, *Sexual Freedom: Urban Erotic Poetry*. The creativity in his books gives him an art of being spiritual and sexual. Mr. Taylor is a student of the human condition, wielding the written craft to enrapture the mind much like an artist wields a brush. The pages are a blank canvas on which to draw from a talent heralded by many and matched only by an imagination that rises to the task. He writes in a rap style of the Apocalypse to destroy all evil forces surrounding him. He resides in DC.

Preview of the Scale of a Libra's Heart

Alphonso Taylor

Infatuation of a Libra

Her name is Talora Jameson, more of a Libra, the diva. It was seven years ago when she met Andre 'Dre' Simms at club, Love formerly known as Dream, which is one of DC's hottest spots. Talora wasn't interested in him, although she thought he was cute. Dre was just a man she didn't want at that time or at least that's what she felt. Dre gave Talora his number and she called two days later as they talked for what seemed like forever. They hooked up for their first date to have dinner at Olive's Garden. After that, because Talora and Dre's schedules were so busy, they came to an agreement just to date once a month and still keep in contact with each other.

Talora didn't really see Dre again until almost a year later, as she was shopping at Wheaton Mall in Maryland with her best friend, Danielle. Talora was looking for the newest shoes in The Coach store. As Talora and Danielle came out the store with hands full of bags, they ran into Dre with his friends, Damien and Jerrod. After introducing one another and small conversation, they all decided to hang out together for the rest of the night. Who would have ever thought on that summer night, Talora will meet the man to fall deeply in love with? Later in those seven years, different women came and disappeared, but Talora remained loyal. The lies, rumors and infidelity got stronger and so did Talora especially running into an old friend, Sedrick Reeves.

Sedrick and Talora went to junior high school together and were in the same class. They were both quite nerds and Sedrick was real short. He used to irritate the shit out of

Talora and always gave her a look like he couldn't stand her ass. She guesses it was because of her sassiness that she still has from those teenage years and him just being a typical boy. It was around the year 2006, when Talora came across Sedrick after all that time on MySpace, a networking and social site for people, which seems like everybody and their momma are on there. She sent him a friend request and he accepted it, although he was still carrying on some baggage from school. Sedrick said Talora used to treat him bad, but she actually felt he was cool and funny as hell. They started talking for awhile, and Sedrick began to let his guard down especially after hearing all the wonderful things they've been doing through Talora's close cousin, JR who also went to school with them too. JR's favorite thing was chasing all the chicks he could muster back in that day.

Soon, Sedrick would become highly attracted to Talora as he tries to keep their friendship the way it is. Still, Sedrick can't fight the unbearable desires he has developed for her. The downside is he just got out of a two year and a half relationship with his fiancé, Vonette. Unfortunately, Sedrick had cheated. As a Libra, Talora has a tendency to maintain balance between men and her. But, as Sedrick constantly pursues her and she still have feelings for Dre, how much can the scale of Talora's heart weigh...?

Alphonso Taylor

Coming Soon in Late 2010 or Early 2011: The Scale of a Libra's Heart

alphonsotaylor.com
www.myspace.com/alphonsotaylor
www.astapublications.com

More of Tiffany 'Parris Jewel' Parker @

www.myspace.com/parrisjewel

More of Donato Sebastian @

www.myspace.com/donatosebast

www.ingramcontent.com/pod-product-compliance
Lightning Source LLC
Chambersburg PA
CBHW031456040426
42444CB00007B/1124